ENGINEERING ANSWERS

How Airplanes Fly

BY TAMMY GAGNE

Kids Core
An Imprint of Abdo Publishing
abdobooks.com

abdobooks.com

Published by Abdo Publishing, a division of ABDO, PO Box 398166, Minneapolis, Minnesota 55439.

Printed in the United States of America, North Mankato, Minnesota.
102024
012025

Cover Photo: Shutterstock Images
Interior Photos: Shutterstock Images, 4–5, 10–11, 15, 16, 18–19, 23, 28–29; LCpl. Jacob Bertram/US Marines/Alamy Live News/US Air Force Photo/Alamy, 7; Llewellyn/Alamy, 8; guvendemir/E+/Getty Images, 12; Albert Beukhof/Shutterstock Images, 20; Tamme Wichmann/Shutterstock Images, 22; Jay Fog/Shutterstock Images, 24; F. Armstrong Photography/Shutterstock Images, 26

Editor: Marley Richmond
Series Designer: Laura Kuchar

Library of Congress Control Number: 2024938374

Publisher's Cataloging-in-Publication Data

Names: Gagne, Tammy, author.
Title: How airplanes fly / by Tammy Gagne
Description: Minneapolis, Minnesota: ABDO Publishing, 2025 | Series: Engineering answers | Includes online resources and index.
Identifiers: ISBN 9781098295844 (lib. bdg.) | ISBN 9798384916840 (ebook)
Subjects: LCSH: Engineering--Juvenile literature. | Airplanes--Juvenile literature. | Flight--Juvenile literature. | Aerospace engineering--Juvenile literature. | Questions and answers--Juvenile literature. | Engineering design--Juvenile literature.
Classification: DDC 620.1--dc23

CONTENTS

A plane must drive to a runway before it can take off. Runways are long stretches of flat ground where planes can gather speed to lift off.

CHAPTER 1

Ready for Takeoff!

The pilot of an Airbus A320 is ready to leave the airport. She asks **air traffic control** for permission to take off. The controller tells her the plane has been cleared to leave the ground. It is the first of many A320s that will take off today.

The aircraft starts speeding down the runway. It rolls on wheels beneath the plane. Powerful engines push the heavy aircraft forward. It weighs about 87 tons (79 metric tons). That is about as much as two fully loaded semitrucks. As the plane speeds up, it starts to lift into the air. The pilot adjusts controls to keep

Smaller Plane, Lower Takeoff Speed

Larger planes need more speed to take off than smaller planes. The Cessna 172 Skyhawk weighs about 1,680 pounds (762 kg). That is a little less than half the weight of an average car. A Cessna 172 Skyhawk needs a speed of only 63 miles per hour (102 km/h) for takeoff.

Some military aircraft have special engines that allow them to rise straight up when taking off.

the plane on the ground. Once it is moving at 170 miles per hour (274 km/h), she allows the plane to lift off the runway. This is the speed an Airbus A320 needs for a safe takeoff.

First, just the nose rises. Then the rest of the plane lifts into the air. The aircraft starts to climb higher. It keeps moving upward. It reaches an **altitude** of 39,000 feet (11,900 m). The pilot will keep the plane at this altitude until she is ready to begin landing.

Boeing 737s are some of the most common passenger planes. A typical 737 can hold up to 215 passengers.

What Are Airplanes?

Airplanes are vehicles that fly in the air. They have fixed wings. This means the wings don't move. Some airplanes are big enough to carry hundreds of people. Others have enough space for only one or two passengers.

The first airplane flight happened in 1903. That plane was called the Wright Flyer. It flew just 120 feet (37 m). Modern planes fly much farther and faster. Most passenger planes today fly at about 575 miles per hour (925 km/h).

Many types of planes share the sky now. Passenger planes take people to destinations all over the world. Cargo planes transport goods such as food and clothing. Military planes help service members fight wars and deliver aid to people who need it.

Further Evidence

Look at the website below. Does it give any new evidence to support Chapter One?

Taking Flight with the Wright Brothers

abdocorelibrary.com/airplanes-fly

Airplanes are heavy. They use a lot of energy to create the force needed to fly. This energy comes from fuel.

CHAPTER 2

The Science of Flight

Four **forces** act on an airplane during flight. They are gravity, lift, thrust, and drag. Each of these forces affects the plane in a different way. A plane must overcome gravity and drag to fly. Lift and thrust make flight possible.

The front edge of an airplane's wing is curved. This curve helps create lift.

Gravity and Lift

Gravity keeps a plane on the ground when it isn't flying. This force pulls objects with **mass** toward each other. Because Earth is so massive, its gravity pulls objects toward the ground. Planes need to overcome gravity to fly.

The upward force that keeps a plane in the air is called lift. This force must be stronger than gravity. Changes in **air pressure** create lift.

Every part of a plane is affected by lift. But most of the lift comes from the wings. The shape of airplane wings makes air move faster over them than underneath them. This lowers the air pressure above the wing. Air pressure beneath the wing increases. The difference in pressure pushes the plane up into the air.

Thrust and Drag

Planes move forward to fly. The force that causes this motion is called thrust. Thrust moves planes down runways. It also allows planes to move forward in the air.

In most cases, an airplane's thrust comes from engines. Jet engines burn fuel to create hot gas. This gas shoots out the back of the engine and causes thrust. Some smaller planes use **propellers** to give thrust. Both engines and propellers push the vehicle forward in motion.

The Third Law of Motion

Isaac Newton (1643–1727) studied how objects move and work. His third law of motion helps explain flight. This law states that for every action, there is an equal and opposite reaction. Airplane wings force air downward. The equal and opposite force of lift pushes the aircraft up.

Some propeller airplanes have one propeller at the front, and some have one on each wing. Smaller planes need less thrust than large airplanes, so they have fewer propellers.

Airplanes experience four forces when flying.

As a plane moves forward, it meets air **resistance**. This force is called drag. Drag slows down a plane. A plane's thrust must be stronger than its drag for the aircraft to fly.

Primary Source

Tejasri Gururaj writes about science. She explained how lift works for airplanes. She said:

> When a plane's engine is turned on, air rapidly flows over the wings, pushing the air toward the ground. This creates an upward force, [called] lift, that balances and overcomes the plane's weight.

Source: Tejasri Gururaj. "How High Can Planes Fly?" *Smore Science*, 16 Nov. 2022, smorescience.com. Accessed 23 Feb. 2024.

Comparing Texts

Think about the quote. Does it support the information in this chapter? Or does it give a different perspective? Explain how in a few sentences.

Pilots have many controls inside a plane. Some of these controls help the pilots steer.

Taking Control

Getting off the ground is just one part of flying. Planes must also stay stable in the air, and pilots must be able to steer. Pilots steer planes and keep them stable by adjusting how air flows along the plane.

Many military fighter jets have small fuselages. This makes these jets lighter than large passenger planes. Military jets can fly very fast because they are light.

Fuselage

The main body of a plane is called the fuselage.

This is the part of the plane that holds people

and cargo. The shape of the fuselage is a bit different for every type of airplane.

Most fuselages are long, round shapes with pointed tips. This design reduces drag on the airplane. Air flows more easily past a rounded fuselage.

The Tail

The tail of an airplane plays a big role in controlling movement. Strong winds often blow against a flying airplane. Wind can cause a plane's nose to move from side to side. This movement is called yaw. A plane's tail fin helps keep the plane stable. The fin keeps air flowing in line with the plane.

The flat wings on an airplane's tail are sometimes called stabilizers. Elevators are flaps on the backs of these stabilizers.

The rudder is on the tail fin. Moving the rudder right or left increases air pressure on one side of the tail. This allows pilots to adjust yaw and keep the plane stable.

Other parts of the tail keep the plane level. Flat wings on the tail control **pitch**. Tail wings have flaps called elevators that pilots can control. These flaps tilt to adjust lift. Moving the elevators can push the plane's nose up or down.

Controlling Yaw

Airplane pilots use the plane's rudder to adjust the yaw of an airplane. Turning the rudder pushes the tail of the airplane to one side and the nose to the other.

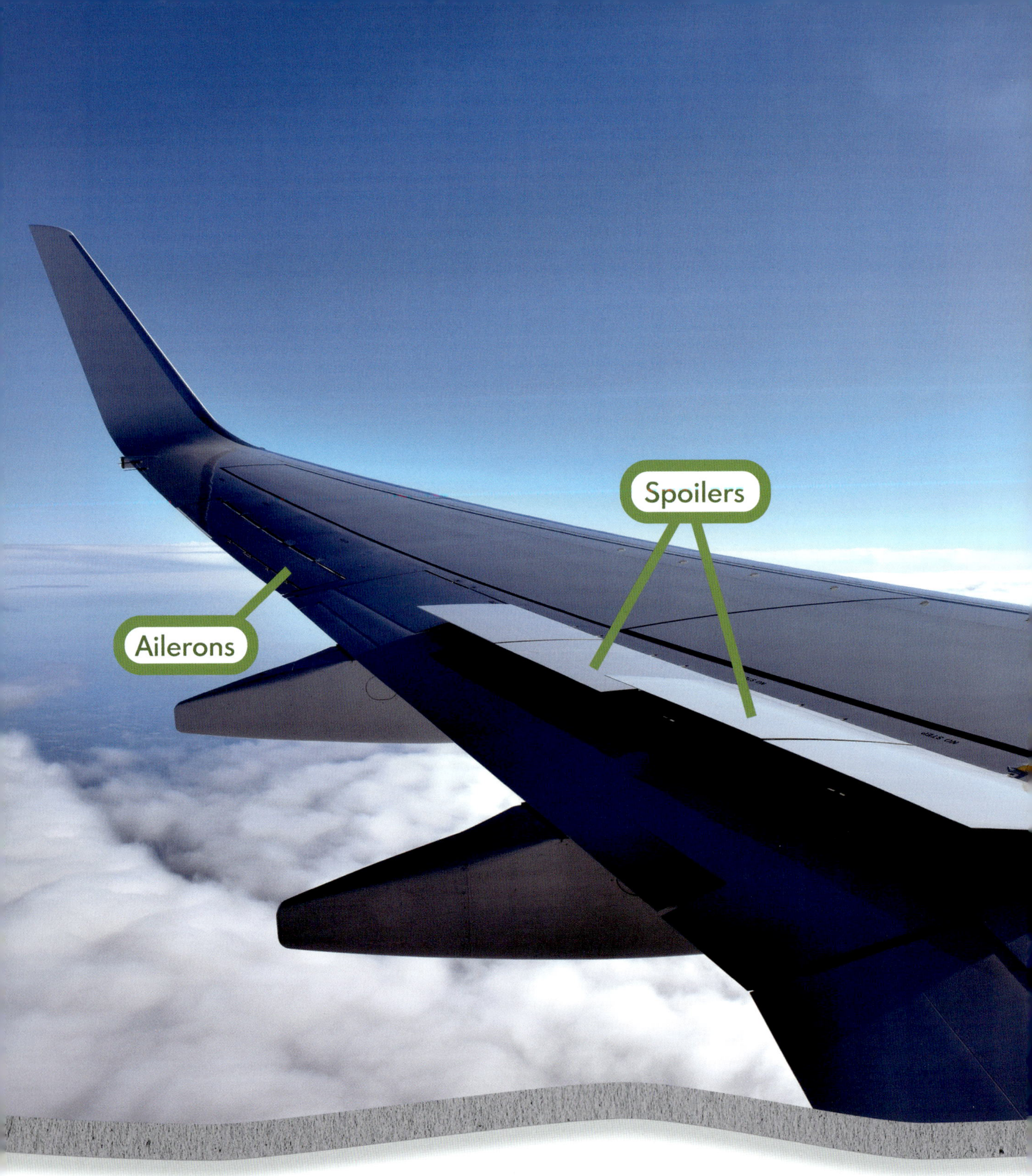

Ailerons are located near the tips of airplane wings. Spoilers are flaps on the tops of wings.

The Wings

A plane also has flaps on each wing. These are called ailerons and spoilers. They keep the plane from rolling to either side. They also help the plane make turns.

Ailerons and spoilers change the amount of lift each wing creates. When these flaps are adjusted, one wing tip creates more lift.

Autopilot Feature

Some planes can fly themselves. Autopilot systems guide planes without input from human pilots at the controls. Long ago, autopilot systems could fly a plane only in a straight and level path through the air. But now, these systems can even land a plane on their own.

When an airplane turns by rolling partway to one side, this is called banking. Ailerons and spoilers are used to bank an airplane.

That wing tip rises. The other moves down. This causes the plane's path to curve toward the wing that is lower.

Airplanes fly through the sky every day. They use lift and thrust to stay in the air. These forces overcome gravity and drag. Pilots keep planes moving safely in the right direction with the help of many tools.

Explore Online

Visit the website below. Does it give any new information about airplanes that wasn't in Chapter Three?

What Are the Parts of an Airplane?

abdocorelibrary.com/airplanes-fly

Engineering Facts

Most of a plane's lift comes from its wings.

The tail plays a big role in controlling a plane's movement.

The fuselage is the main body of the plane.
A plane's engines are usually below its wings.

Glossary

air pressure
the force of air pressing against a surface

air traffic control
a network of workers who direct airplanes and other flying vehicles on the ground and in the air

altitude
height above sea level

force
a push or pull that transfers energy into an object

mass
the amount of matter in an object

pitch
the degree or angle of a slope

propeller
a spinning device with blades attached to it

resistance
an opposing force

Online Resources

To learn more about how airplanes fly, visit our free resource websites below.

Visit **abdocorelibrary.com** or scan this QR code for free Common Core resources for teachers and students, including vetted activities, multimedia, and booklinks, for deeper subject comprehension.

Visit **abdobooklinks.com** or scan this QR code for free additional online weblinks for further learning. These links are routinely monitored and updated to provide the most current information available.

Learn More

Holzweiss, Kristina A. *My First Book of Airplanes.* Rockridge, 2022.

Lamichhane, Priyanka. *Planes.* Abdo, 2024.

Ringstad, Arnold. *How Rockets Reach Space.* Abdo, 2025.

Index

About the Author

Tammy Gagne is an author and editor who specializes in nonfiction. She has written hundreds of books for both children and adults. She lives in northern New England with her husband, son, and dogs.